In recognition of a gift to the

Opening the Door to the Future
Capital Campaign
for the Falmouth Public Library
2006 - 2008

From

Edith Anne Fredericks

Thank You!

J
PICTURE
Kerley

J
PICTURE
Kerley

A *little*
PEACE

by Barbara Kerley

with a note by Richard H. Solomon
President, United States Institute of Peace

NATIONAL GEOGRAPHIC
WASHINGTON, D.C.

All it takes is…

one HAND

One SMILE

A single VOICE

To *give* a **WAVE**

Say HELLO

And *spread* a little PEACE

At the **MARKET**

Down the STREET

On a crowded BUS

Or a sandy **BEACH**

During WORSHIP

PRAYER

MEDITATION

During **STUDY**

PLAY

CELEBRATION

Joining NEIGHBORS

Making **FRIENDS**

From **HOME** to **HOME**
and **SHORE** to **SHORE**

Share your **SMILE**

Lend a **HAND**

Spread a little **PEACE**

A little PEACE around the WORLD

Arctic Ocean

NORTH AMERICA

ASIA

EUROPE

Edinburgh, Scotland
London, England
Padova, Italy
Kabul, Afghanistan
Tokyo, Japan
Mazar-e Sharif, Afghanistan
Leh, Ladakh, India
Baghdad, Iraq
Al Kūt, Iraq
Srinagar, Kashmir, India
Fengdu, China
Kathmandu, Nepal
Gazipur, Bangladesh
Trashi Yangtse, Bhutan
Dover, Ohio, U.S.A.
Brooklyn, New York, U.S.A.
Albuquerque, New Mexico, U.S.A.
New Orleans, Louisiana, U.S.A.

Atlantic Ocean

Basse-Terre, Guadeloupe
Shendi, Sudan
AFRICA
Pacific Ocean

Chichicastenango, Guatemala

Pacific Ocean

SOUTH AMERICA
Salvador, Brazil

Kitale, Kenya

Mekong Delta, Vietnam

Bali, Indonesia

Indian Ocean

AUSTRALIA

0 — 3000 miles
0 — 4000 kilometers

ANTARCTICA

Front cover:

GAZIPUR, BANGLADESH
A boy smiles as he rests on a boat floating in a rice paddy. The Bangladeshi constitution affirms human rights, with respect for the dignity and worth of all people.
PHOTOGRAPH BY RASHED ZAMAN

ALBUQUERQUE, NEW MEXICO, U.S.A.
Children in a line hold hands as they play together. PHOTOGRAPH BY STEPHEN MARKS/THE IMAGE BANK/GETTY IMAGES

DOVER, OHIO, U.S.A.
A four-year-old girl expresses herself. Freedom of speech was guaranteed by the Bill of Rights in 1791. PHOTOGRAPH BY DAVID ROTH/STONE/GETTY IMAGES

KATHMANDU, NEPAL
In a moment of quiet, a girl holds a small bouquet. Traditionally, a Nepali host welcomes an honored guest with a gift of marigolds. PHOTOGRAPH BY RIC ERGENBRIGHT

BALI, INDONESIA
A group of schoolchildren wave in Bali. Indonesia's national motto, *Bhineka Tunggal Ika*, reflects the country's diversity: "They are different, but they are one." PHOTOGRAPH BY MARK KATZMAN/HALO IMAGES

NEAR KITALE, KENYA
A beautiful smile lights up the face of a Pokot girl. More than 70 ethnic groups live within Kenya's borders. PHOTOGRAPH BY ERIC L. WHEATER/LONELY PLANET IMAGES

LONDON, ENGLAND
Two men tip their hats to say hello. The custom is thought to have originated during the Middle Ages, when knights raised their visors as a sign of friendship. PHOTOGRAPH BY WILL & DENI MCINTYRE/CORBIS

CHICHICASTENANGO, GUATEMALA
Shoppers enjoy small pockets of peace amid the bustle of market day. The city is famous for its large and colorful outdoor market, where people gather to shop. PHOTOGRAPH BY CARSTEN SNEJBJERG/WORLD PICTURE NEWS

PADOVA, ITALY
Cobblestones make for a bumpy ride on a bicycle just big enough for two. The city is home to the University of Padua, where students from all over the world come to study. PHOTOGRAPH BY LOU JONES/LONELY PLANET IMAGES

OUTSIDE SHENDI, SUDAN
Sudanese share news and stories on a bus going to the market town of Shendi. Founded by shepherds, the town is named for the Daju word *chendé*, which means "sheep." PHOTOGRAPH BY NIGEL PAVITT/JOHN WARBURTON-LEE PHOTOGRAPHY

BASSE-TERRE, GUADELOUPE
Two boys play in the surf, sand, and sun. Many people come to the beach to relax and spend time with friends. PHOTOGRAPH BY BRUNO MORANDI

NEW ORLEANS, LOUISIANA, U.S.A.
Choir members sing and clap hands as they worship through joyful music. Damaged in 2005 during Hurricane Katrina, the Greater St. Stephen Church is committed to rebuilding the community. PHOTOGRAPH BY BOB SACHA/CORBIS

SRINAGAR, KASHMIR, INDIA
Men pray in a mosque during Ramadan, a month-long holiday that includes time for contemplation and for strengthening bonds between neighbors. PHOTOGRAPH BY AMI VITALE

TRASHI YANGTSE, BHUTAN
Buddhist monks perform a whirling, meditative dance. The practice deepens their understanding and aids spiritual growth. PHOTOGRAPH BY AMI VITALE

FENGDU, CHINA
Seated at an outdoor desk, a young girl studies under the watchful eye of her grandmother. Schools in China teach subjects such as language and math and also values such as the importance of truth and kindness. PHOTOGRAPH BY JUSTIN GUARIGLIA

BAGHDAD, IRAQ
Despite the presence of an Iraqi tank, a stark reminder of war, young men come together in a moment of boisterous play. PHOTOGRAPH BY BENJAMIN LOWY/CORBIS

SALVADOR, BRAZIL
Dancers parade down the streets to celebrate Fat Tuesday, the highlight of Carnival season. This holiday, which features music, feasting, and costumes, is celebrated in countries around the world. PHOTOGRAPH BY PETER ADAMS/ZEFA/CORBIS

BROOKLYN, NEW YORK, U.S.A.
On a hot July day, the spray of an open fire hydrant cools neighborhood children. The borough prides itself on its rich ethnic diversity. PHOTOGRAPH BY MARY ALTAFFER/ASSOCIATED PRESS

KABUL, AFGHANISTAN
Two friends relax in the marketplace while waiting to begin work. After years of political turmoil, the country recently held its first democratic election. PHOTOGRAPH BY TOMAS MUNITA

LEH, LADAKH, INDIA
A young boy and his friends enjoy an afternoon of freedom after being released from school. People from India, Tibet, and China have settled in this region, one of the highest places in the world. PHOTOGRAPH BY RIC ERGENBRIGHT

TOKYO, JAPAN
A young boy lends a hand by pushing the crosswalk button. In Japan, children are cherished, especially as the general population ages rapidly. PHOTOGRAPH BY B.S.P.I./CORBIS

MEKONG DELTA, VIETNAM
A girl smiles as she flashes the peace sign. After struggling through years of war, Vietnam is now thriving in peacetime. PHOTOGRAPH BY KRISTA KENNELL/ZUMA/CORBIS

AL KŪT, IRAQ
A doctor with the United States Marine Corps comforts an Iraqi boy after fighting between American and Iraqi soldiers. PHOTOGRAPH BY DAMIR SAGOLJ/REUTERS/CORBIS

EDINBURGH, SCOTLAND
Girls carry a banner as they call for peace. Thousands of schoolchildren all over Britain rallied in 2003 to protest the war in Iraq. PHOTOGRAPH BY JEFF J. MITCHELL/REUTERS/CORBIS

Back cover:

MAZAR-E SHARIF, AFGHANISTAN
An old man feeds the pigeons near the Shrine of Hazrat Ali on the first day of the Eid Festival, celebrating the end of Ramadan. Around the world, white birds are a symbol of peace. PHOTOGRAPH BY TOMAS MUNITA/ASSOCIATED PRESS

A note on PEACE

President Franklin D. Roosevelt said, "More than an end to war, we want an end to the beginning of all wars." The United States Institute of Peace was founded by the American Congress to pursue that world-changing goal. We are an independent, nonpartisan, national institution. We work to end violent conflicts and foster peace around the world. We study conflict situations, sponsor training in conflict resolution skills, give grants for researchers and teachers, and support policymakers. As part of our educational outreach, we host a summer training institute on issues of war and peace for teachers, and we sponsor an annual peace essay contest for high school students in every state of our country. As an organization, we teach citizens that the responsibility to work for peace does not rest with governments and organizations alone; it is also the work of individuals.

Lao Tzu (570–490 B.C.), a famous Chinese philosopher, wrote:

If there is to be peace in the world,

> **PEACE** cannot be kept by *force.* It can only be achieved by *understanding.*
>
> —ALBERT EINSTEIN, 1930

There must be peace among nations.
If there is to be peace among nations,
There must be peace in the cities.
If there is to be peace in the cities,
There must be peace between neighbors.
If there is to be peace between neighbors,
There must be peace in the home.
If there is to be peace in the home,
There must be peace in the heart.

CRADLED IN A MOMENT OF FLEETING PEACE
A marine holds a child who was separated from his family after a battle in Iraq. All too often, children are the innocent victims of war.

In my work as a peace negotiator, I have helped resolve conflicts in Cambodia and Vietnam, and worked to end nuclear proliferation on the Korean Peninsula. I've traveled much of the world, and I've spoken with people from many different countries and ethnic groups about the conflicts in their lives. I've been a witness to the misunderstandings and differences that divide people, that if not managed well can lead to conflict. I've seen the terrible costs of war! But I've also seen, even more powerfully, how we as a human family have a great desire for peace. Today, more than ever, we need peace among peoples and nations, and in our personal lives.

To achieve that peace, we need to empower governments and organizations to foster creative peace-making activities around the world. We also need to help individuals develop the skills to be peacemakers.

One of the most powerful tools in the promotion of peace is education. Education can promote the values of tolerance, mutual understanding, and respect for others. It can unlock the peace that lies in our hearts.

One of the programs that the Institute of Peace has supported is "Seeds of Peace." This peace education program brings together Israeli and Palestinian teenagers for a six-week educational summer camp in Maine. The program's goal is to foster mutual understanding and friendships, and prevent young people from becoming enemies. Seeds of Peace teaches the arts of peacemaking to the next generation of Israeli and Palestinian leaders. Its motto, like this book, is simple and powerful: "Treaties are negotiated by governments. Peace is made by people."

The pictures and words you've seen and read in these pages make clear just how much we share with our global human family the desire for peace. Each one of us is striving for peace in our lives, for mutual understanding and friendship. When we find it, we can share it. "All it takes is one hand, one smile, a single voice...." Through education and our personal efforts, we can each spread a little peace. And then we can have the joy of watching it grow. So, learn to be a peacemaker!

There was never a good **WAR** *or a* **bad PEACE.**

—BEN FRANKLIN, 1783

All we are saying is *give* **PEACE** a **CHANCE.**

—JOHN LENNON, 1969

RICHARD H. SOLOMON, President
United States Institute of Peace

For **DEB**

Published by the National Geographic Society.

Special thanks to Jennifer Emmett, Lori Epstein, and Bea Jackson

If you would like to learn more about the United States Institute of Peace,
visit: http://www.usip.org/ or call 202-429-4144.

Book Designer: Bea Jackson
Design Intern: Mike Robbins
Illustrations Editor: Lori Epstein
The text of the book is set in Mrs. Eaves and Trade Gothic.

Library of Congress Cataloging-in-Publication Data
Kerley, Barbara.
A little peace / by Barbara Kerley ; with a note by Richard H. Solomon.
p. cm.
Includes bibliographical references and index.
ISBN-13: 978-1-4263-0086-8 (hardcover : alk. paper)
ISBN-13: 978-1-4263-0087-5 (lib. bdg. : alk. paper)
1. Peace--Juvenile literature. 2. Peace--Pictorial works--Juvenile literature. I. Title. II. Title: Peace.
JZ5560.K47 2006
327.1'72--dc22

2006026367

One of the world's largest nonprofit scientific and educational organizations, the National Geographic Society was founded in 1888 "for the increase
and diffusion of geographic knowledge." Fulfilling this mission, the Society educates and inspires millions every day through its magazines, books,
television programs, videos, maps and atlases, research grants, the National Geographic Bee, teacher workshops, and innovative classroom materials.
The Society is supported through membership dues, charitable gifts, and income from the sale of its educational products. This support is vital to
National Geographic's mission to increase global understanding and promote conservation of our planet through exploration, research, and education.

For more information, please call 1-800-NGS-LINE (647-5463) or write to the following address:
NATIONAL GEOGRAPHIC SOCIETY
1145 17th Street N.W.
Washington, D.C. 20036-4688 U.S.A.
Visit the Society's Web site: www.nationalgeographic.com

PRINTED IN THE UNITED STATES OF AMERICA